Table of Contents

Introduction: The Ketogenic Lifestyle

Welcome to "Ketogenic Versions of Traditional Indian Meals" – a recipe book that explores the fusion of the ketogenic diet with the rich and diverse flavours of Indian cuisine. In this book, we will embark on a culinary journey that brings the health benefits of the ketogenic lifestyle to the vibrant tapestry of Indian dishes.

The ketogenic diet, or keto diet, is a low-carb, high-fat diet that has gained popularity for its ability to promote weight loss, improve mental clarity, and enhance energy levels. By limiting carbohydrates and increasing the consumption of healthy fats, our bodies enter a state of ketosis, where we burn fats for fuel rather than carbohydrates.

India, known for its aromatic spices and mouth-watering curries, has a culinary heritage that spans centuries. It is challenging to imagine the Indian diet without its staple ingredients like rice, lentils, and various flours. However, with a little culinary creativity and smart ingredient substitutions, we can adapt traditional Indian meals to fit within the framework of the ketogenic lifestyle.

In Chapter 1, we will delve into the benefits of the ketogenic diet and explore how Indian cuisine can be modified to fit this way of eating. We will discuss how you can embrace the keto lifestyle and the positive impact it can have on your health and well-being. Moreover, we will explore strategies for adapting beloved Indian dishes to adhere to the principles of the ketogenic diet.

The subsequent chapters will take you on a gastronomic adventure through a variety of meal categories, including breakfasts, appetisers, mains, salads, desserts, and beverages. Each chapter will present four carefully curated recipes that showcase the marriage of authentic Indian flavours with keto-friendly ingredients.

Our aim is to inspire you to explore the possibilities of Indian cuisine while nourishing your body with the principles of the ketogenic diet. We have carefully selected recipes that balance taste, nutritional value, and the uniqueness of Indian cooking.

Before diving into the recipes, you'll find an informative glossary of Indian spices and a list of keto-friendly Indian superfoods in the appendices. Additionally, we offer practical tips for maintaining the delicate balance between ketosis and the wonderful flavours of Indian cooking.

Whether you are a newcomer to the ketogenic diet, a seasoned chef looking for inventive recipes, or an Indian food enthusiast seeking healthier alternatives, this book will be your reliable guide to transforming everyday Indian meals into keto-friendly delights.

Let's embark on this flavourful adventure and discover the joys of a ketogenic lifestyle intertwined with the familiarity of beloved Indian dishes. Together, we can redefine what it means to balance health and tradition in the kitchen.

Embrace the Keto Lifestyle

In this introductory chapter, we will delve into the fascinating world of the ketogenic diet and its compatibility with the flavoursome realm of Indian cuisine. Here, we will explore the benefits of the ketogenic lifestyle, understand the science behind it, and discover how we can adapt traditional Indian meals to align with this dietary approach.

The ketogenic diet has gained significant recognition for its ability to promote weight loss, increase energy levels, and improve mental clarity. By drastically reducing our intake of carbohydrates and replacing them with healthy fats, we encourage our bodies to enter a state of ketosis. In this state, our metabolism shifts, and we begin to burn stored fat for energy, leading to the desirable process of weight loss.

Indian cuisine has long been celebrated for its array of aromatic spices, vibrant colours, and a harmonious blend of flavours. However, traditional Indian meals often heavily rely on ingredients high in carbohydrates, such as rice, lentils, and various flours. The challenge lies in reimagining these dishes and adapting them to fit the principles of the ketogenic diet without compromising on taste and authenticity.

In this chapter, we will explore how you can embrace the keto lifestyle while still enjoying the essence of Indian cuisine. We will delve into the specific benefits that the ketogenic diet offers and shed light on how it can positively impact your overall well-being. With a focus on mindful ingredient choices and thoughtful substitutions, we will show you how to transform your beloved Indian meals into keto-friendly versions that do not compromise on taste or cultural identity.

We will also provide practical tips and tricks for adapting your kitchen practices and pantry essentials to accommodate the ketogenic lifestyle. From sourcing quality ingredients to understanding the nutritional value of different foods, we will equip you with the necessary knowledge to embark on this exciting culinary journey.

By the end of this chapter, you will have a solid grasp of the fundamental principles behind the ketogenic diet and an understanding of how those principles can be integrated into the Indian culinary landscape. You will be ready to embark on the rest of the book, where we will explore a variety of delicious and keto-friendly Indian recipes across different meal categories.

Get ready to embrace the keto lifestyle and revolutionize your relationship with Indian cuisine. Let's embark on this journey together, where tradition meets innovation, and health takes centre stage.

Understanding the Benefits of the Ketogenic Diet

The ketogenic diet has gained immense popularity in recent years, and for good reason. In this segment, we will delve into the numerous benefits that the ketogenic lifestyle offers, providing you with the motivation and understanding to embrace this dietary approach.

Weight Loss: One of the primary reasons people turn to the ketogenic diet is its effectiveness in promoting weight loss. By drastically reducing carbohydrate intake and increasing the consumption of healthy fats, our bodies become efficient at burning stored fat for energy. This can lead to significant weight loss over time, while still providing us with the necessary nutrients and energy to thrive.

Steady Energy Levels: Unlike the highs and lows associated with a high-carbohydrate diet, the ketogenic diet aims to provide a steady supply of energy throughout the day. By relying on fats for fuel instead of carbohydrates, we can reduce blood sugar fluctuations and the subsequent energy crashes. This can result in increased focus, improved productivity, and a more stable mood throughout the day.

Enhanced Mental Clarity: Ketones, substances produced by the liver during ketosis, are known to provide a stable and efficient energy source for the brain. Many individuals report improved mental clarity, increased concentration, and enhanced cognitive function while following the ketogenic diet. This can be particularly beneficial for those who require sustained mental performance, such as students or professionals.

Controlled Blood Sugar Levels: The ketogenic diet has been shown to have a positive impact on blood sugar regulation. By reducing carbohydrate intake, we can minimize spikes in blood sugar levels, making it an attractive option for individuals with diabetes or insulin resistance. However, it is important to consult with a healthcare professional before making any significant dietary changes if you have an underlying health condition.

Reduced Inflammation: Chronic inflammation is increasingly recognized as a key factor in the development of various health conditions, including cardiovascular disease, diabetes, and certain cancers. Studies have suggested that the ketogenic diet may have anti-inflammatory properties, potentially reducing the risk of inflammation-related issues and promoting overall well-being.

Improved Heart Health: While traditionally associated with a high-fat intake, the ketogenic diet focuses on consuming healthy fats, such as avocados, nuts, and fatty fish. This approach can lead to an improvement in various markers of heart health, including cholesterol levels, triglyceride levels, and blood pressure. However, as with any dietary changes, it is crucial to ensure a well-rounded and balanced approach.

By understanding the benefits of the ketogenic diet, you can gain valuable insight into why this lifestyle has captured the attention of many health-conscious individuals. Embracing the ketogenic diet can potentially transform your overall well-being, promoting weight loss, enhancing mental and physical performance, and supporting various aspects of your health.

In the next segment, we will explore how these benefits can be adapted to the unique characteristics of Indian cuisine, enabling you to enjoy the flavours and cultural heritage while aligning with the principles of the ketogenic diet. Let's uncover the possibilities of a ketogenic Indian culinary adventure in the following segment.

Adapting to the Keto Lifestyle

Embracing the ketogenic lifestyle doesn't mean you have to bid farewell to the vibrant and aromatic world of Indian cuisine. In this segment, we will explore practical strategies and tips for adapting traditional Indian meals to align with the principles of the ketogenic diet.

Mindful Ingredient Choices: The key to successfully adapting Indian recipes to fit the ketogenic lifestyle lies in making mindful ingredient choices. Look for low-carbohydrate alternatives to traditional ingredients, such as replacing rice with cauliflower rice or using almond flour instead of wheat flour for rotis or flatbreads. By exploring these ingredient substitutions, you can still enjoy the essence of Indian cuisine while adhering to the principles of the ketogenic diet.

Focusing on Healthy Fats: The ketogenic diet emphasizes the consumption of healthy fats, which play a vital role in providing sustained energy and supporting overall health. Embrace fats like avocados, coconut oil, ghee (clarified butter), and fatty cuts of meat. These fats not only add depth and richness to your dishes but also keep you feeling satisfied for longer periods of time.

Balancing Protein Intake: While the ketogenic diet places a greater emphasis on fats, it is also essential to maintain a balanced protein intake. Opt for protein sources like lean meats, fish, eggs, and dairy products to ensure you meet your protein requirements. In Indian cooking, dishes like tandoori chicken, paneer tikka, or fish curry can be excellent choices to incorporate protein while keeping carbohydrates in check.

Using Spices and Herbs: Indian cuisine is renowned for its bold and aromatic use of spices and herbs. Fortunately, many of these spices, such as turmeric, cumin, coriander, and fenugreek, are not only flavorful but also offer various health benefits. They can assist with digestion, reduce inflammation, and provide a natural boost to your immune system. Embrace these spices and herbs to enhance the taste and nutritional value of your ketogenic Indian meals.

Experimenting with Vegetable Alternatives: One of the great advantages of Indian cuisine is its wide range of vegetable-based dishes. Embrace low-carbohydrate vegetables like spinach, cauliflower, broccoli, and zucchini to create satisfying and nutrient-rich dishes. For example, try using cauliflower rice instead of traditional rice in biryanis or saag paneer made with spinach instead of high-carb greens. These versatile vegetables can be incorporated into a variety of dishes while keeping your carbohydrate intake in check.

Portion Control and Mindful Eating: While adapting Indian dishes to the ketogenic lifestyle, it is also important to practice portion control and mindful eating. Even with keto-friendly ingredients, overeating can hinder progress and weight loss. Be mindful of your portion sizes and listen to your body's signals of hunger and fullness.

Remember, adapting to the ketogenic lifestyle with Indian cuisine is a journey of exploration and creativity. It may require some trial and error to find the perfect balance of flavours and ingredients that resonate with your taste buds and align with your dietary goals. Adaptation and flexibility are key to enjoying the delicious and diverse world of Indian food while following the principles of the ketogenic diet.

In the next segment, we will delve into the fusion of the ketogenic diet and the vibrant world of Indian cuisine, where we will explore a selection of mouth-watering and keto-friendly recipes across different meal categories. So, get ready to embark on a culinary adventure that brings together the best of both worlds.

Indian Cuisine and the Ketogenic Diet

Indian cuisine is a treasure trove of rich flavours, aromatic spices, and diverse culinary traditions. From fragrant curries to mouth-watering street food, it has captivated taste buds around the world. In this segment, we will explore how Indian cuisine can be adapted to harmonize with the principles of the ketogenic diet, while still keeping its unique essence intact.

Embracing the Flavours: Indian cuisine is renowned for its vibrant and bold flavours, derived from a delightful blend of spices, herbs, and aromatics. The good news is that many of these spices are low in carbohydrates and can be freely enjoyed on a ketogenic diet. Spices like turmeric, cumin, coriander, and garam masala not only add depth and complexity to dishes but also offer various health benefits. By incorporating these aromatic spices into your ketogenic Indian recipes, you can enjoy the explosion of flavours while staying true to the principles of the diet.

Carbohydrate Awareness: Traditional Indian meals often rely heavily on carbohydrate-rich ingredients like rice, lentils, and flours. However, with a little creativity, you can find keto-friendly alternatives that still provide the texture and satisfaction you crave. For instance, using cauliflower rice instead of regular rice or almond flour instead of wheat flour allows you to enjoy familiar dishes while keeping your carbohydrate intake in check. By being mindful of the carbohydrate content of ingredients, you can modify recipes to fit the ketogenic lifestyle without sacrificing taste.

Healthy Fat Substitutions: Indian cooking traditionally includes the usage of cooking oils such as vegetable oil or ghee. When following a ketogenic diet, it is important to focus on consuming healthy fats. By substituting these oils with options like coconut oil, avocado oil, or ghee, you can maintain authenticity while aligning with the principles of the ketogenic diet. These healthy fat alternatives not only enhance the taste of your dishes but also provide important nutrients to support your overall well-being.

Vegetarian and Vegan Options: Indian cuisine offers a diverse range of vegetarian and vegan dishes, making it well-suited for those who follow a plant-based ketogenic diet. With the abundance of vegetables, legumes, and dairy substitutes available, you can create keto-friendly versions of beloved Indian vegetarian dishes. For instance, replacing paneer with tofu or coconut milk for dairy-based curries can offer a delicious plant-based alternative without compromising on taste or nutritional balance.

Balancing Macros: Balancing macronutrients is an essential aspect of the ketogenic diet. While Indian cuisine can be rich in carbohydrates, it also offers a variety of protein and fat sources. By carefully selecting your ingredients and portion sizes, you can create meals that strike the right balance of macronutrients to support ketosis. Be mindful of your protein and fat intake, ensuring they are in line with your specific dietary goals.

Adapting Indian cuisine to the ketogenic diet allows you to enjoy the rich tapestry of flavours and diverse regional specialties while reaping the benefits of this eating style. With an understanding of how to make thoughtful ingredient choices, embrace healthy fats, and adapt traditional recipes, you can confidently embark on this culinary adventure.

In the upcoming chapters, we will explore a range of ketogenic recipes that will showcase the fusion of Indian cuisine and the ketogenic lifestyle. Get ready to tantalize your taste buds with mouth-watering breakfasts, appetisers, main courses, desserts, and beverages, all designed to bring the magic of Indian flavours to your ketogenic journey.

Kickstart Your Mornings: Keto-friendly Indian Breakfasts

Rise and shine! In this chapter, we dive into the vibrant world of breakfast, where we showcase a delectable array of keto-friendly Indian dishes to kickstart your day. From fluffy omelettes to warm and comforting dosas, get ready to indulge in the flavours and nourishment of an Indian breakfast with a low-carb twist.

Breakfast is often hailed as the most important meal of the day, setting the tone for our energy levels and overall well-being. With keto-friendly Indian breakfast options, you can fuel your body with wholesome ingredients while satisfying your taste buds.

In this chapter, we present four carefully curated recipes that showcase the versatility and indulgence of Indian breakfasts adapted for the ketogenic lifestyle. Each recipe has been meticulously crafted to ensure it is low in carbohydrates, high in healthy fats, and bursting with authentic Indian flavours.

Start your day with a Keto Masala Omelette, a fluffy and flavourful creation packed with protein and an aromatic blend of spices. Or savour the delightful fusion of a Keto Rasam Soup with Almond Flour Dosa, where the tangy and spiced flavours of rasam meet the delightful crispness of a dosa made with almond flour.

For those who desire something different, try our Coconut Flour Upma, a comforting and satisfying dish made with cauliflower, bell peppers, and Indian spices, all enhanced with the subtle sweetness of coconut flour. And let's not forget our twist on a classic with Cauliflower Poha, a hearty and flavourful dish that replaces rice flakes with cauliflower rice, ensuring you stay comfortably within your low-carb limits.

By exploring these keto-friendly Indian breakfast recipes, you can discover new ways to enjoy the aromatic spices, comforting textures, and invigorating flavours of Indian cuisine while adhering to the principles of the ketogenic diet. These recipes are designed to nourish your body, ignite your taste buds, and set you up for a productive and satisfying day ahead.

So, grab your apron, heat up the skillet, and get ready to indulge in a mouth-watering breakfast experience. Join us as we explore the fusion of Indian breakfast traditions with the low-carb delights of the ketogenic lifestyle. From savoury to mildly sweet, we have something to appease every palate and add a touch of excitement to your mornings.

In the next chapter, we continue our culinary adventure through the realm of Indian cuisine, exploring a variety of tempting appetisers with a keto-friendly twist. Get ready to tantalize your taste buds as we unravel the secrets to creating delectable and health-conscious Indian starters.

Keto Masala Omelette

Ingredients:
- 3 large eggs
- 1 tablespoon heavy cream
- 1/4 cup diced onions
- 1/4 cup diced bell peppers
- 1 green chili, finely chopped (optional, for heat)
- 1/4 teaspoon turmeric powder
- 1/4 teaspoon cumin powder
- 1/4 teaspoon red chili powder
- Salt, to taste
- 2 tablespoons ghee (clarified butter), for cooking
- Fresh coriander leaves, for garnish

Instructions:
1. In a bowl, crack the eggs and add the heavy cream. Whisk the mixture until well combined and slightly frothy.
2. Add the diced onions, bell peppers, green chili (if using), turmeric powder, cumin powder, red chili powder, and salt to the egg mixture. Mix everything together until the vegetables and spices are evenly distributed.
3. Heat a non-stick frying pan over medium heat and add the ghee. Allow it to melt and coat the bottom of the pan.
4. Pour the egg mixture into the pan, spreading it evenly to cover the surface. Cook for 2-3 minutes until the edges start to set.
5. Using a spatula, gently lift the edges of the omelette and tilt the pan to let the uncooked egg mixture flow to the edges.
6. Cook for another 2-3 minutes or until the omelette is cooked through and slightly golden on the bottom.
7. Carefully flip the omelette over and cook for an additional 1-2 minutes or until the other side is cooked to your desired level of doneness.
8. Transfer the omelette to a serving plate and garnish with fresh coriander leaves.
9. Serve the Keto Masala Omelette hot as a standalone breakfast dish or pair it with a side of keto-friendly bread or vegetables for a more substantial meal.

Enjoy the delightful combination of eggs, aromatic spices, and colourful vegetables in this keto-friendly twist on a classic Indian breakfast. The Keto Masala Omelette is a perfect way to start your day with a protein-packed and flavourful dish that will leave you feeling satisfied and energized.

Keto Rasam Soup with Almond Flour Dosa

Keto Rasam Soup Ingredients:
- 2 tomatoes, chopped
- 1 small tamarind pulp, soaked in water (about 1 teaspoon)
- 2 cups water
- 1/2 teaspoon cumin seeds
- 1/2 teaspoon black peppercorns
- 1/2 teaspoon turmeric powder
- 1/2 teaspoon ghee (clarified butter)
- A pinch of asafoetida (optional)
- Salt, to taste
- Fresh coriander leaves, for garnish

Almond Flour Dosa Ingredients:
- 1 cup almond flour
- 1 tablespoon ground flaxseed
- 1/2 teaspoon cumin seeds
- 1/2 teaspoon salt
- 1 cup water (approximately)

Instructions:

Keto Rasam Soup:
1. In a blender, blend the tomatoes to a smooth puree.
2. In a saucepan, heat the ghee over medium heat. Add the cumin seeds and black peppercorns, and sauté until fragrant.
3. Stir in the tomato puree and cook for a couple of minutes until the raw smell of tomatoes disappears.
4. Add the turmeric powder, asafoetida (if using), and tamarind pulp water (strained from the soaked tamarind) to the pan. Mix well.
5. Pour in the water and season with salt. Stir to combine.
6. Reduce the heat to low and simmer the rasam soup for about 10-15 minutes, allowing the flavours to meld together.
7. Garnish with fresh coriander leaves before serving.

Almond Flour Dosa:
1. In a mixing bowl, combine the almond flour, ground flaxseed, cumin seeds, and salt.
2. Gradually add water to the mixture, whisking continuously until you achieve a smooth batter consistency. The batter should be thin enough to spread easily but not watery.
3. Heat a non-stick skillet or dosa pan over medium heat. Grease it lightly with ghee.
4. Pour a ladleful of the batter onto the skillet, then quickly spread it into a thin, circular shape using the back of the ladle.
5. Cook the dosa for a couple of minutes until the edges turn golden brown and the surface is crisp.
6. Flip the dosa and cook on the other side for a minute or so until golden.
7. Repeat the process with the remaining batter.

Serve the Keto Rasam Soup hot with the Almond Flour Dosa on the side. Dip the dosa into the rasam to enjoy the delightful combination of tangy and spiced flavours. This keto-friendly rendition of a beloved Indian classic is a perfect way to warm yourself up and satisfy your cravings for traditional Indian flavours without compromising your low-carb lifestyle.

Coconut Flour Upma

Ingredients:
- 1 cup cauliflower rice
- 2 tablespoons coconut flour
- 1 tablespoon ghee (clarified butter)
- 1 teaspoon mustard seeds
- 1 teaspoon cumin seeds
- 1 small onion, finely chopped
- 1 green chili, finely chopped (optional, for heat)
- 1/4 cup diced bell peppers
- 1/4 cup green peas
- 1/4 teaspoon turmeric powder
- Salt, to taste
- Fresh coriander leaves, for garnish

Instructions:
1. In a skillet, heat the ghee over medium heat. Add the mustard seeds and cumin seeds. Let them sizzle for a few seconds until fragrant.
2. Add the finely chopped onion and green chili to the skillet. Sauté until the onion turns translucent and light golden brown.
3. Stir in the diced bell peppers and green peas. Cook for a few minutes until the vegetables are slightly tender.
4. Add the cauliflower rice to the skillet and mix well with the vegetables.
5. Sprinkle turmeric powder and salt over the mixture. Stir to distribute the spices evenly.
6. Reduce the heat to low and cover the skillet. Allow the mixture to cook for about 5-7 minutes, or until the cauliflower rice is cooked and the flavours have melded together.
7. Remove the lid and sprinkle coconut flour over the mixture. Mix well to incorporate the flour into the dish, ensuring it absorbs any excess moisture.
8. Cook for an additional 2-3 minutes until the coconut flour is cooked through.
9. Garnish with fresh coriander leaves before serving.

Enjoy this keto-friendly Coconut Flour Upma as a satisfying and flavourful Indian breakfast option. The combination of cauliflower rice, aromatic spices, and the nutty taste of coconut flour creates a delightful and low-carb twist on a beloved Indian dish. Savour its comforting textures, vibrant colours, and authentic flavours as you savor each bite.

Cauliflower Poha

Ingredients:
- 1 small cauliflower, grated or riced
- 1 tablespoon ghee (clarified butter)
- 1/2 teaspoon mustard seeds
- 1/2 teaspoon cumin seeds
- 1 small onion, finely chopped
- 1 green chili, finely chopped (optional, for heat)
- 1/4 cup roasted peanuts
- 1/4 cup green peas
- A handful of curry leaves
- 1/4 teaspoon turmeric powder
- Salt, to taste
- Fresh coriander leaves, for garnish
- Lemon wedges, for serving

Instructions:
1. Heat the ghee in a large skillet or pan over medium heat. Add the mustard seeds and cumin seeds. Let them sizzle for a few seconds until fragrant.
2. Add the finely chopped onion and green chili to the skillet. Sauté until the onion turns translucent and light golden brown.
3. Stir in the grated or riced cauliflower, roasted peanuts, green peas, and curry leaves. Mix well to combine all the ingredients.
4. Sprinkle turmeric powder and salt over the mixture. Stir to evenly coat the cauliflower and vegetables with the spices.
5. Reduce the heat to low and cover the skillet. Allow the mixture to cook for about 5-7 minutes, or until the cauliflower is tender and cooked through.
6. Remove the lid and give the cauliflower poha a gentle stir. Adjust the seasoning if necessary.
7. Garnish with fresh coriander leaves and serve hot with a squeeze of lemon juice for added freshness.

Indulge in this keto-friendly version of Cauliflower Poha, a beloved Indian breakfast dish made with cauliflower instead of traditional rice flakes. Experience the familiar blend of flavours and textures, with the added bonus of being low in carbs and high in nutrients. Enjoy the comforting cauliflower, the crunch of roasted peanuts, and the aromatic spices that make this dish a satisfying breakfast choice. Squeeze some lemon juice over it for a tangy kick that perfectly complements the flavours.

Mid-day Munchies: Keto Indian Appetisers

Welcome to the appetising world of Indian cuisine, where we explore a collection of tantalising keto-friendly Indian appetisers. In this chapter, we will delve into the vibrant and diverse realm of Indian starters, showcasing a selection of low-carb twists on beloved dishes that will excite your taste buds and set the stage for a memorable meal.

Appetisers hold a special place in Indian culinary traditions, offering a burst of flavours and textures that awaken the palate and prepare us for the forthcoming feast. Now, with our keto-friendly adaptations, you can indulge in the enticing flavours and aromatic spices of Indian appetisers without veering away from your low-carb eating habits.

In this chapter, we present four carefully crafted recipes that demonstrate the fusion of authentic Indian flavours with the principles of the ketogenic diet. From succulent Paneer Tikka to the hearty Mushroom Ghee Roast, each recipe has been meticulously designed to be low in carbohydrates and high in deliciousness.

We begin with Paneer Tikka, a popular Indian appetiser that combines cubes of paneer cheese marinated in a tantalising blend of spices and cooked to perfection. Then, we tantalise your taste buds with our Spinach Tikki, a delightful low-carb twist on the traditional potato-based tikki, featuring a mix of spinach and spices, pan-fried until golden and crispy.

Next, we present the Mushroom Ghee Roast, a flavourful and aromatic dish where earthy mushrooms are sautéed in ghee and a medley of spices for a mouth-watering experience. Finally, we introduce you to our keto-friendly Samosas, where a crispy and golden almond flour-based pastry engulfs a spiced and delicious filling. These bite-sized wonders will transport you to the bustling streets of India, all while keeping your carbohydrate intake in check.

In this chapter, you will discover how to create tantalising appetisers that not only align with your ketogenic goals but also capture the essence of Indian cuisine. These recipes will impress your guests, delight your taste buds, and leave you craving more.

So, as you immerse yourself in the world of Keto Indian Appetisers, prepare to embark on a flavourful journey that brings together the best of both worlds. Get ready to enjoy the vibrant and diverse appetisers of Indian cuisine while staying firmly on your low-carb path to wellness.

Paneer Tikka

Ingredients:
- 250 grams paneer (Indian cottage cheese), cut into cubes
- 1/4 cup plain Greek yogurt
- 1 tablespoon ginger-garlic paste
- 1 tablespoon lemon juice
- 1 teaspoon Kashmiri red chili powder (or paprika)
- 1/2 teaspoon turmeric powder
- 1/2 teaspoon cumin powder
- 1/2 teaspoon garam masala
- 1/2 teaspoon chaat masala
- Salt, to taste
- 1 tablespoon ghee (clarified butter), for cooking
- Fresh coriander leaves, for garnish
- Lemon wedges, for serving

Instructions:
1. In a bowl, combine Greek yogurt, ginger-garlic paste, lemon juice, Kashmiri red chili powder, turmeric powder, cumin powder, garam masala, chaat masala, and salt. Mix well to make a marinade.
2. Add the paneer cubes to the marinade and gently toss until each cube is coated evenly. Allow the paneer to marinate for at least 30 minutes in the refrigerator, allowing the flavours to meld.
3. Preheat the grill or a non-stick frying pan on medium-high heat. If using a frying pan, add the ghee and allow it to melt.
4. Skewer the marinated paneer cubes onto skewers, leaving a little space between each cube.
5. Grill the paneer skewers or cook them in the frying pan for about 2-3 minutes on each side, until the paneer is lightly charred and golden.
6. Remove the paneer tikka skewers from the grill or pan and transfer them to a serving plate.
7. Garnish with fresh coriander leaves and serve hot with lemon wedges on the side.

Paneer Tikka is a classic Indian appetiser loved for its smoky, spicy, and aromatic flavours. With this keto-friendly recipe, you can enjoy this delightful dish while keeping your carbohydrate intake in check. The tender and succulent paneer, marinated in a harmonious blend of spices and grilled to perfection, will leave you wanting more. Serve it as an appetiser at parties or enjoy it as a tasty snack any time of the day. The bright and tangy lemon wedges add a refreshing touch, enhancing the overall experience. Prepare to be dazzled by the flavours of this Paneer Tikka delight!

Spinach Tikki

Ingredients:
- 2 cups spinach, blanched and finely chopped
- 1/2 cup grated paneer (Indian cottage cheese)
- 1/4 cup finely chopped onions
- 2 green chilies, finely chopped
- 1/2 teaspoon ginger paste
- 1/2 teaspoon garlic paste
- 1/2 teaspoon garam masala
- 1/2 teaspoon cumin powder
- 1/2 teaspoon red chili powder
- Salt, to taste
- 1 tablespoon almond flour
- 2 tablespoons ghee (clarified butter), for cooking
- Fresh coriander leaves, for garnish
- Lemon wedges, for serving

Instructions:
1. In a large bowl, combine the chopped spinach, grated paneer, finely chopped onions, green chilies, ginger paste, garlic paste, garam masala, cumin powder, red chili powder, salt, and almond flour. Mix well until all the ingredients are thoroughly combined.
2. Divide the mixture into equal portions and shape each portion into a round patty or tikki.
3. Heat ghee in a non-stick frying pan over medium heat. Place the tikkis in the pan and cook for about 3-4 minutes on each side, or until they turn golden brown and crisp.
4. Once cooked, transfer the tikkis to a paper towel-lined plate to absorb any excess oil.
5. Garnish with fresh coriander leaves and serve hot with lemon wedges on the side.

Spinach Tikki is a delightful keto-friendly twist on the classic Indian potato tikki. Packed with nutritious spinach, protein-rich paneer, and a medley of aromatic spices, these tikkis offer a burst of flavour and a satisfying crunch. The tikkis are pan-fried to perfection, giving them a lovely golden exterior. Perfect as an appetiser or a light snack, they can be enjoyed on their own or served with a dollop of mint chutney or a squeeze of lemon juice for that added tanginess. These Spinach Tikkis are bound to impress both keto enthusiasts and lovers of Indian cuisine alike with their deliciousness and low-carb goodness.

Mushroom Ghee Roast

Ingredients:
- 250 grams mushrooms, cleaned and sliced
- 1 tablespoon ghee (clarified butter)
- 1 teaspoon mustard seeds
- 1 teaspoon cumin seeds
- 1 large onion, thinly sliced
- 2 green chilies, slit lengthwise
- 1 sprig curry leaves
- 1 tablespoon ginger-garlic paste
- 1 teaspoon turmeric powder
- 1 teaspoon red chili powder
- 1 teaspoon coriander powder
- 1/2 teaspoon garam masala
- Salt, to taste
- Fresh coriander leaves, for garnish
- Lemon wedges, for serving

Instructions:
1. In a large frying pan, heat the ghee over medium heat. Add the mustard seeds and cumin seeds and let them splutter.
2. Add the sliced onions, green chilies, and curry leaves to the pan. Sauté until the onions become translucent and lightly browned.
3. Stir in the ginger-garlic paste and cook for a minute until the raw aroma disappears.
4. Add the turmeric powder, red chili powder, coriander powder, garam masala, and salt. Mix well and cook for a minute to allow the spices to release their flavours.
5. Add the sliced mushrooms to the pan and stir-fry until they are cooked through and slightly caramelised, about 8-10 minutes.
6. Once the mushrooms are cooked, remove the pan from the heat.
7. Garnish the Mushroom Ghee Roast with fresh coriander leaves and serve hot with lemon wedges on the side.

Mushroom Ghee Roast is a heavenly combination of earthy mushrooms, aromatic spices, and rich ghee that creates a flavourful experience like no other. This keto-friendly appetiser is a tantalising blend of textures and tastes, with the mushrooms caramelising in the spices and ghee for a mouth-watering result. Indulge in the aromatic and bold flavours of this dish, complemented by the freshness of coriander leaves and a squeeze of tangy lemon juice. Whether served as an appetiser or a side dish, Mushroom Ghee Roast is sure to impress with its delightful flavours and keto-friendly ingredients.

Keto-friendly Samosas

Ingredients:
For the pastry:
- 1 cup almond flour
- 1/4 cup coconut flour
- 1/4 teaspoon salt
- 2 tablespoons ghee (clarified butter), melted
- 1/4 cup warm water

For the filling:
- 1 cup cauliflower, finely chopped
- 1/4 cup green peas
- 1/4 cup finely chopped onions
- 1 green chili, finely chopped
- 1/2 teaspoon ginger paste
- 1/2 teaspoon garlic paste
- 1/2 teaspoon turmeric powder
- 1/2 teaspoon cumin powder
- 1/2 teaspoon coriander powder
- 1/4 teaspoon red chili powder
- Salt, to taste
- 2 tablespoons ghee (clarified butter), for cooking

Instructions:
1. In a large mixing bowl, combine almond flour, coconut flour, and salt for the pastry. Mix well.
2. Add melted ghee to the dry ingredients and mix until crumbly.
3. Gradually add warm water, 1 tablespoon at a time, and knead the mixture into a smooth dough. Cover the dough and set it aside to rest for 15 minutes.
4. Meanwhile, prepare the filling. Steam or boil the cauliflower florets and green peas until tender. Drain any excess water and set aside.
5. In a frying pan, heat ghee over medium heat. Add the chopped onions, green chili, ginger paste, and garlic paste. Sauté until the onions turn translucent.
6. Stir in the turmeric powder, cumin powder, coriander powder, red chili powder, and salt. Cook for a minute to allow the spices to release their aromas.
7. Add the steamed cauliflower and green peas to the pan. Mix well, allowing the vegetables to absorb the flavors of the spices. Cook for another 2-3 minutes. Remove from heat and let the filling cool.
8. Preheat the oven to 350°F (180°C). Line a baking sheet with parchment paper.
9. Divide the dough into small equal portions and roll each portion into a thin circle on a lightly greased surface.
10. Cut the rolled dough into semi-circles. Take each semi-circle and fold it into a cone, sealing the edges with a little water.
11. Fill each cone with a spoonful of the cooled cauliflower and pea filling. Seal the top of the cone tightly.
12. Place the samosas on the prepared baking sheet. Brush the tops with melted ghee.
13. Bake for 20-25 minutes, or until the samosas turn golden brown and crisp.

14. Remove from the oven and let them cool slightly before serving.

These keto-friendly samosas are the perfect appetiser or snack for those following a low-carb lifestyle. The almond and coconut flour pastry offers a deliciously flaky texture, while the spiced cauliflower and pea filling adds a burst of flavour. Enjoy these crispy, golden triangles of delight guilt-free, either on their own or with a side of mint chutney or sugar-free ketchup. Prepare to be transported to the streets of India with every bite, as you savour the phenomenal taste of these keto samosas.

Get Your Curry On: Hearty Indian Keto Mains

Prepare your taste buds for a culinary adventure in Chapter 4, where we delve into the heart of Indian cuisine and present a selection of hearty ketogenic Indian mains. From rich and creamy curries to succulent tandoori delights, this chapter offers an array of dishes that celebrate the bold flavours and traditional favourites of Indian cuisine, all while staying low-carb.

Indian cuisine is renowned for its aromatic spices, diverse regional specialties, and a harmonious blend of ingredients. In this chapter, we bring the magic of Indian cooking to your ketogenic lifestyle, ensuring that you can enjoy the robust and satisfying mains without breaking your low-carb commitment.

Within these pages, you will discover four carefully curated recipes that showcase the fusion of Indian flavours and the principles of the ketogenic diet. Each dish has been meticulously crafted to capture the essence of traditional Indian mains while incorporating keto-friendly ingredients to ensure you can relish the culinary treasures guilt-free.

Indulge in the velvety texture and exquisite taste of Keto Butter Chicken, where tender chicken simmers in a luscious tomato and cream-based sauce enriched with aromatic spices. Or venture into the realm of vegetarian delights with Spinach and Paneer Keto Curry, a dish that combines the earthy flavours of spinach and the creamy richness of paneer cheese.

For seafood lovers, we present the Keto-friendly Fish Curry, a mouth-watering blend of delicate fish cooked in a spicy and tangy curry sauce. And for those seeking a spicy kick, explore the robust flavours of Lamb Vindaloo with Cauliflower Rice, a fiery curry dish that will delight your taste buds and satisfy your craving for bold and aromatic flavours.

Whether you are a seasoned cook or just starting out on your culinary journey, these ketogenic Indian mains will add a touch of flair to your mealtime repertoire. From the complexity of the spices to the depth of the flavors, each dish invites you to savor the rich heritage of Indian cuisine while staying true to your low-carb lifestyle.

So, dust off your spice rack, fire up your stove, and get ready to embark on a flavourful adventure through the captivating world of Indian ketogenic mains. These dishes will not only fill your home with enticing aromas but also nourish your body and transport you to the vibrant streets of India. Let's get your curry on and explore the heartiness and deliciousness of Indian cuisine redesigned for the ketogenic diet.

Keto Butter Chicken

Ingredients:
- 500g boneless chicken, cut into bite-sized pieces
- 2 tablespoons ghee (clarified butter) or cooking oil
- 1 large onion, finely chopped
- 3 cloves garlic, minced
- 1-inch ginger, grated
- 2 tomatoes, chopped
- 1/4 cup heavy cream
- 1/4 cup Greek yogurt
- 1 teaspoon turmeric powder
- 1 teaspoon cumin powder
- 1 teaspoon coriander powder
- 1/2 teaspoon paprika
- 1/2 teaspoon red chili powder (adjust to taste)
- 1/2 teaspoon garam masala
- Salt, to taste
- Fresh coriander leaves, for garnish

Instructions:
1. Heat the ghee or cooking oil in a large skillet over medium heat. Add the chopped onion and sauté until it turns golden brown and translucent.
2. Add the minced garlic and grated ginger to the skillet. Cook for an additional minute until fragrant.
3. Add the chopped tomatoes to the skillet and cook until they soften and release their juices, stirring occasionally.
4. In a small bowl, mix together the turmeric powder, cumin powder, coriander powder, paprika, red chili powder, and garam masala.
5. Add the spice mixture to the skillet with the onions, garlic, and tomatoes. Stir well to coat the ingredients and cook for a minute to toast the spices.
6. Add the chicken pieces to the skillet and cook until they are browned on all sides, stirring occasionally to ensure even cooking.
7. Reduce the heat to low and stir in the heavy cream and Greek yogurt. Simmer for 10-15 minutes, allowing the flavors to meld together and the chicken to become tender.
8. Season with salt to taste, and adjust the spiciness if desired by adding more red chili powder.
9. Remove from heat and garnish with fresh coriander leaves.
10. Serve the Keto Butter Chicken hot with cauliflower rice or low-carb naan bread for a satisfying and indulgent meal.

Savor the richness and creamy deliciousness of this Keto Butter Chicken, a beloved classic of Indian cuisine adapted for your low-carb lifestyle. Tender chicken bathing in a luscious tomato and cream-based sauce, infused with aromatic spices, creates a tantalizing dish that will transport your taste buds to new heights. With every bite, you'll enjoy the depth of flavors and the comforting richness of this keto-friendly version. Revel in this culinary delight while embracing your ketogenic journey.

Lamb Vindaloo with Cauliflower Rice

Ingredients:
- 500g boneless lamb, cut into bite-sized pieces
- 1 large cauliflower, riced
- 2 tablespoons ghee (clarified butter) or cooking oil
- 1 large onion, finely chopped
- 4 cloves garlic, minced
- 1-inch ginger, grated
- 2 teaspoons garam masala
- 1 teaspoon turmeric powder
- 1 teaspoon cumin powder
- 1 teaspoon coriander powder
- 1 teaspoon paprika
- 1 teaspoon red chili powder (adjust to taste)
- 1/2 cup tomato puree
- 1/4 cup apple cider vinegar
- 1/4 cup water (adjust as needed)
- Salt, to taste
- Fresh coriander leaves, for garnish

Instructions:
1. Heat the ghee or cooking oil in a large skillet or pot over medium heat. Add the chopped onion and sauté until golden brown and caramelized.
2. Add the minced garlic and grated ginger to the skillet and cook for an additional minute until fragrant.
3. In a small bowl, mix together the garam masala, turmeric powder, cumin powder, coriander powder, paprika, and red chili powder.
4. Add the spice mixture to the skillet with the caramelized onions, garlic, and ginger. Stir well to coat the onions and spices.
5. Add the diced lamb to the skillet and cook until browned on all sides, stirring occasionally to ensure even cooking.
6. Pour in the tomato puree, apple cider vinegar, and water. Stir to combine all the ingredients and bring the mixture to a simmer.
7. Reduce the heat to low, cover the skillet, and let the lamb simmer for approximately 1 hour or until it becomes tender and the flavors meld together.
8. While the lamb is simmering, prepare the cauliflower rice by pulsing the cauliflower florets in a food processor until they resemble rice grains.
9. In a separate pan, heat a little ghee or oil and add the cauliflower rice. Sauté for a few minutes until it softens slightly but still retains some texture.
10. Season the cauliflower rice with salt to taste.
11. Once the lamb is tender, adjust the seasoning with salt and any additional spices if desired.
12. Serve the Lamb Vindaloo over a bed of cauliflower rice and garnish with fresh coriander leaves for added freshness and aroma.

Get ready to tantalize your taste buds with this Keto-friendly version of the classic Indian Lamb Vindaloo. The tender and flavorful lamb, combined with the aromatic spices and tangy tomato sauce, creates a symphony of flavors that will transport your senses to the streets of India. Enjoy this delicious and satisfying low-carb meal that perfectly balances the richness of the curry with the lightness of cauliflower rice, offering you the best of both worlds.

Spinach and Paneer Keto Curry

Ingredients:
- 200g paneer, cubed
- 300g spinach leaves, washed and chopped
- 1 tablespoon ghee (clarified butter) or cooking oil
- 1 large onion, finely chopped
- 3 cloves garlic, minced
- 1-inch ginger, grated
- 1 teaspoon cumin seeds
- 1 teaspoon coriander powder
- 1/2 teaspoon turmeric powder
- 1/2 teaspoon red chili powder (adjust to taste)
- 1/4 teaspoon garam masala
- 1/4 cup heavy cream
- Salt, to taste
- Fresh coriander leaves, for garnish

Instructions:
1. Heat the ghee or cooking oil in a large skillet over medium heat. Add the cumin seeds and let them splutter for a few seconds.
2. Add the chopped onion to the skillet and sauté until it turns golden brown and translucent.
3. Add the minced garlic and grated ginger to the skillet. Cook for an additional minute until fragrant.
4. Stir in the coriander powder, turmeric powder, and red chili powder. Cook for a minute to toast the spices and release their flavors.
5. Add the chopped spinach to the skillet and cook until it wilts down, stirring occasionally to ensure even cooking.
6. Add the cubed paneer to the skillet and gently stir to combine it with the spinach and spices.
7. Pour in the heavy cream, stirring well to coat the paneer and spinach mixture. Simmer for a few minutes until the sauce thickens slightly.
8. Season with salt to taste and sprinkle in the garam masala. Stir well to incorporate all the flavors.
9. Cover the skillet and let the curry simmer over low heat for 5-7 minutes, allowing the paneer to absorb the flavors of the sauce.
10. Remove from heat and garnish with fresh coriander leaves.
11. Serve the Spinach and Paneer Keto Curry hot with cauliflower rice or a side of low-carb bread for a satisfying and healthy meal.

Indulge in the lush and creamy goodness of this Spinach and Paneer Keto Curry. The combination of nutrient-rich spinach, tender paneer, and aromatic spices creates a harmonious symphony of flavors that is delicious and keto-friendly. This low-carb adaptation of a classic Indian dish is not only packed with taste but also provides a nourishing and satisfying meal. Enjoy this wholesome and comforting curry that celebrates the beauty of Indian cuisine while supporting your ketogenic lifestyle.

Keto-friendly Fish Curry

Ingredients:
- 500g white fish fillets (such as cod or tilapia)
- 2 tablespoons ghee (clarified butter) or cooking oil
- 1 large onion, finely chopped
- 3 cloves garlic, minced
- 1-inch ginger, grated
- 2 tomatoes, chopped
- 1 teaspoon turmeric powder
- 1 teaspoon cumin powder
- 1 teaspoon coriander powder
- 1/2 teaspoon red chili powder (adjust to taste)
- 1/2 teaspoon paprika
- 1/4 cup coconut milk
- 1/4 cup water (adjust as needed)
- Salt, to taste
- Fresh coriander leaves, for garnish

Instructions:
1. Heat the ghee or cooking oil in a large skillet over medium heat. Add the chopped onion and sauté until it turns golden brown and translucent.
2. Add the minced garlic and grated ginger to the skillet. Cook for an additional minute until fragrant.
3. Add the chopped tomatoes to the skillet and cook until they soften and release their juices, stirring occasionally.
4. In a small bowl, mix together the turmeric powder, cumin powder, coriander powder, red chili powder, and paprika.
5. Add the spice mixture to the skillet with the onions, garlic, and tomatoes. Stir well to coat the ingredients and cook for a minute to toast the spices.
6. Place the fish fillets into the skillet, nestling them into the sauce. Gently spoon the sauce over the fish to ensure even coating.
7. Pour in the coconut milk and water, and season with salt to taste. Stir gently to combine all the ingredients.
8. Cover the skillet and let the fish simmer over low heat for 10-15 minutes, or until the fish is cooked through and flakes easily with a fork.
9. Remove from heat and garnish with fresh coriander leaves.
10. Serve the Keto-friendly Fish Curry hot with cauliflower rice or low-carb naan bread for an authentic Indian culinary experience.

Dive into the delightful flavors of this Keto-friendly Fish Curry, where tender fish is enveloped in a fragrant and creamy sauce. This low-carb adaptation of a classic Indian dish is a seafood lover's dream, combining the freshness of fish with aromatic spices and the richness of coconut milk. Indulge in the unique blend of flavors while staying true to your ketogenic lifestyle. Enjoy this delicious and nourishing fish curry that captures the essence of Indian cuisine in a healthy and satisfying way.

Light and Breezy: Keto Indian Salads and Sides

In this chapter, we venture into the refreshing realm of salads and sides, where we showcase a delectable selection of keto-friendly Indian dishes that will add a burst of flavour and nutrition to your meals. From crunchy salads to mouth-watering vegetable sides, get ready to discover the lighter side of Indian cuisine with a low-carb twist.

Salads and sides are often overlooked in Indian cuisine, but they play a vital role in enhancing the overall dining experience. With keto-friendly Indian salads and sides, you can elevate your meals with vibrant colours, textures, and a multitude of flavours while staying true to your keto lifestyle.

In this chapter, we present four carefully curated recipes that combine the best of both worlds - the health-conscious nature of salads and sides with the authentic tastes of Indian cuisine. Each recipe has been thoughtfully crafted to provide a balance of fresh ingredients, zesty dressings, and the aromatic spices that are synonymous with Indian cooking.

Immerse yourself in the unique tang of a Kongunadu Salad, where crisp vegetables are combined with a tantalizing blend of spices and a refreshing dressing. Or, indulge in the Keto Tandoori Cauliflower, an explosion of flavours where roasted cauliflower meets the enticing smokiness of tandoori spices, making it the perfect side dish for any meal.

For a delightful crunch, try the Spiced Keto Okra Fry, a dish that combines the earthiness of okra with a delightful kick of spices and a satisfying texture. And if you crave the rice-based goodness of biryani, opt for the Keto Bombay Biryani Style Cabbage - a creative and low-carb twist on the classic, using cabbage as a substitute for rice.

With these keto-friendly Indian salads and sides, you can elevate your meal planning, add a burst of freshness, and enjoy the health benefits of incorporating nutrient-rich vegetables and spices into your diet. These recipes are designed to provide a well-rounded dining experience, ensuring you can savor the complexities of Indian cuisine without compromising your commitment to a low-carb lifestyle.

So, get ready to mix and match vibrant ingredients, experiment with zesty dressings, and explore the diverse range of textures and flavours that Indian salads and sides have to offer. Let's uncover the light and breezy side of Indian cuisine through the lens of the ketogenic diet.

In the upcoming chapter, we will delve into the realm of sweet indulgence as we explore a variety of keto-friendly Indian desserts that will satisfy your cravings while keeping you on track with your low-carb journey. Get ready to enjoy the treats of Indian sweets in a guilt-free and delicious way.

Kongunadu Salad

Ingredients:
- 1 cup chopped cucumber
- 1 cup chopped tomatoes
- 1/2 cup chopped onions
- 1/2 cup grated carrot
- 1/4 cup chopped bell peppers (assorted colours)
- 1 green chili, finely chopped (optional, for heat)
- 2 tablespoons fresh cilantro, chopped
- 1/2 teaspoon chaat masala
- 1/4 teaspoon roasted cumin powder
- 1/4 teaspoon black salt
- Juice of 1 lime
- Salt, to taste

Instructions:
1. In a large bowl, combine the chopped cucumber, tomatoes, onions, grated carrot, bell peppers, and green chili (if using).
2. Add the fresh cilantro to the bowl and gently toss the ingredients together.
3. In a small bowl, prepare the dressing by mixing the chaat masala, roasted cumin powder, black salt, lime juice, and a pinch of salt.
4. Drizzle the dressing over the salad mixture and toss well to ensure all the vegetables are coated.
5. Adjust the seasoning to taste with additional salt or lime juice if desired.
6. Let the salad sit for a few minutes to allow the flavours to meld together.
7. Serve the refreshing Kongunadu Salad as a standalone salad or as a side dish accompanying your favourite Indian meal.

Enjoy the crunch and freshness of this Kongunadu Salad, packed with a harmonious blend of colourful vegetables and tantalizing spices. It is the perfect accompaniment to any keto-friendly Indian meal, bringing vitality and a burst of tangy and zesty flavours to your dining experience.

Keto Tandoori Cauliflower

Ingredients:
- 1 medium cauliflower, cut into florets
- 2 tablespoons plain Greek yogurt
- 1 tablespoon tandoori masala
- 1 teaspoon ginger-garlic paste
- 1 teaspoon lemon juice
- 1/2 teaspoon turmeric powder
- 1/2 teaspoon paprika
- 1/2 teaspoon salt
- 1 tablespoon ghee (clarified butter), melted
- Fresh cilantro, for garnish
- Lemon wedges, for serving

Instructions:
1. Preheat the oven to 200°C (400°F) and line a baking sheet with parchment paper.
2. In a mixing bowl, combine the Greek yogurt, tandoori masala, ginger-garlic paste, lemon juice, turmeric powder, paprika, and salt. Mix well to form a smooth marinade.
3. Add the cauliflower florets to the marinade and gently toss until they are well coated.
4. Allow the cauliflower to marinate for at least 15-20 minutes to allow the flavours to penetrate.
5. Place the marinated cauliflower florets onto the prepared baking sheet in a single layer.
6. Drizzle the melted ghee over the cauliflower florets, ensuring they are evenly coated.
7. Roast in the preheated oven for 20-25 minutes or until the cauliflower is tender and lightly charred around the edges.
8. Remove from the oven and garnish with fresh cilantro.
9. Serve the Keto Tandoori Cauliflower as a flavourful side dish, accompanied by lemon wedges for an extra citrusy kick.

Enjoy the tantalizing aroma and smoky flavors of this Keto Tandoori Cauliflower dish, where the classic Indian tandoori spices infuse through the tender florets of cauliflower. This low-carb and keto-friendly side dish adds a burst of vibrancy to any meal and complements a variety of other Indian dishes with its delightful tang and spice.

Spiced Keto Okra Fry

Ingredients:
- 2 cups fresh okra, trimmed and cut into 1-inch pieces
- 1 tablespoon ghee (clarified butter) or coconut oil
- 1 teaspoon mustard seeds
- 1 teaspoon cumin seeds
- 1/2 teaspoon turmeric powder
- 1/2 teaspoon red chili powder
- 1/2 teaspoon coriander powder
- 1/2 teaspoon salt, or to taste
- Fresh cilantro, for garnish

Instructions:
1. Heat ghee or coconut oil in a large skillet or frying pan over medium heat.
2. Add the mustard seeds and cumin seeds to the pan, and let them sizzle for a few seconds until they start to pop.
3. Add the fresh okra to the pan and stir well to coat the pieces with the seeds and oil.
4. Sprinkle turmeric powder, red chili powder, coriander powder, and salt over the okra, stirring gently to evenly distribute the spices.
5. Stir-fry the okra for 8-10 minutes, or until it is tender and lightly browned. Be careful not to overcook, as we want to maintain a slight crunch.
6. Remove from heat and transfer the spiced keto okra fry to a serving dish.
7. Garnish with fresh cilantro leaves.
8. Serve the Spiced Keto Okra Fry as a delightful side dish with your favourite keto Indian meal or as a crispy and nutritious snack.

Indulge in the delightful crunch and earthy flavors of this Spiced Keto Okra Fry. With its aromatic spices and tender-crisp texture, this low-carb side dish brings a burst of flavor and a touch of heat to your table. Enjoy it as a healthy and satisfying addition to your ketogenic Indian meal or simply relish it as a nutritious snack on its own.

Keto Bombay Biryani Style Cabbage

Ingredients:
- 2 cups shredded cabbage
- 1/2 cup diced onion
- 1/2 cup diced bell peppers (assorted colors)
- 2 tablespoons ghee (clarified butter) or coconut oil
- 1 teaspoon ginger-garlic paste
- 1 green chili, slit lengthwise (optional, for heat)
- 2 teaspoons biryani masala powder
- 1/2 teaspoon turmeric powder
- 1/2 teaspoon red chili powder
- 1/2 teaspoon cumin seeds
- Salt, to taste
- Fresh cilantro, for garnish
- Lemon wedges, for serving

Instructions:
1. Heat ghee or coconut oil in a large skillet or frying pan over medium heat.
2. Add the cumin seeds to the pan and let them sizzle for a few seconds until they release their aroma.
3. Add the diced onion, bell peppers, ginger-garlic paste, and green chili (if using) to the pan. Sauté until the onions turn translucent and the vegetables are slightly softened.
4. Stir in the biryani masala powder, turmeric powder, red chili powder, and salt. Cook for an additional minute to toast the spices and enhance their flavors.
5. Add the shredded cabbage to the pan and toss well to coat it evenly with the spice mixture. Cook for 5-7 minutes, or until the cabbage is tender yet still retains a slight crunch.
6. Adjust the seasoning with additional salt if needed.
7. Garnish the Keto Bombay Biryani Style Cabbage with fresh cilantro.
8. Serve as a flavorful and low-carb side dish alongside your favorite keto Indian mains or enjoy it as a satisfying standalone dish.
9. Squeeze fresh lemon juice over the cabbage just before serving for an added burst of tanginess.

Savor the aromatic flavors and innovative twist of this Keto Bombay Biryani Style Cabbage. With its tender-crisp texture and fragrant blend of spices, this low-carb version of the classic biryani transports you to the streets of Bombay. Enjoy it as a delightful side dish, paired with lemon wedges for a zesty kick, or as a substantial meal on its own, filling your plate with the flavors of India while staying true to your keto lifestyle.

Sweet Tooth Cravings: Keto Indian Desserts

Indulge in a guilt-free paradise of sweetness and satisfy your cravings with our delectable selection of keto-friendly Indian desserts. In this chapter, we bring you a collection of tantalizing sweet treats that will tickle your taste buds, while still keeping you firmly on track with your ketogenic lifestyle.

Desserts hold a special place in our hearts, and we believe that being on a keto diet doesn't mean missing out on the joy of indulging in something sweet. With a clever balance of low-carb ingredients and natural sugar substitutes, we have created a variety of mouth-watering Indian desserts that will delight both your palate and your commitment to healthy living.

In this chapter, you will discover the art of creating keto-friendly Indian desserts that capture the essence of traditional favourites. From the soft and syrupy Gulab Jamun to the rich and creamy Saffron Almond Keto Barfi, each recipe has been thoughtfully crafted to ensure that you can enjoy the sweetness you crave without sacrificing your health goals.

We have also reimagined classics like Coconut Laddoos with Stevia, where the natural sweetness of coconut combines harmoniously with the delightful flavours of cardamom and nuts. And for those who yearn for a comforting and familiar treat, we present a Keto-friendly Indian Rice Pudding that embraces the creamy and fragrant qualities of the beloved traditional dessert.

These keto Indian desserts are not only delicious but also showcase the versatility and adaptability of Indian cuisine when it comes to low-carb alternatives. By exploring the magic of ingredients like almond flour, coconut flour, and sugar substitutes, we have managed to create desserts that are mouth-watering, satisfying, and aligned with the principles of the ketogenic diet.

So, get ready to indulge without guilt as we take you on a journey through a collection of keto-friendly Indian desserts. Treat yourself to the sweet melodies of cardamom, the velvety richness of almond and coconut, and the nostalgic comfort of traditional Indian sweets, all while staying true to your commitment to a healthier lifestyle.

In the following pages, we invite you to explore the world of sweet sensations reimagined for the keto lifestyle. From celebration-worthy treats to simple yet satisfying desserts, this chapter is a paradise for every sweet tooth craving the best of both worlds — the irresistible joy of desserts with the benefits of keto.

Keto-friendly Gulab Jamun

Ingredients:
For the gulab jamun balls:
- 1 cup almond flour
- 1/4 cup coconut flour
- 1/4 cup unsweetened shredded coconut
- 1/4 cup powdered erythritol or your preferred sugar substitute
- 1 teaspoon baking powder
- 1/4 teaspoon cardamom powder
- Pinch of saffron strands (optional)
- 1/4 cup ghee (clarified butter), melted
- 2 tablespoons heavy cream
- 1 teaspoon rose water
- Ghee or coconut oil, for frying

For the sugar-free syrup:
- 1 cup water
- 1 cup powdered erythritol or your preferred sugar substitute
- 1/2 teaspoon rose water
- 4-5 cardamom pods, lightly crushed

Instructions:
1. In a mixing bowl, combine the almond flour, coconut flour, shredded coconut, powdered erythritol, baking powder, cardamom powder, and saffron strands (if using).
2. Add the melted ghee, heavy cream, and rose water to the dry ingredients. Mix well until a dough-like consistency forms. If the dough seems too dry, add a little more heavy cream.
3. Divide the dough into small portions and shape them into smooth, round balls. Make sure to compact the dough well to prevent the balls from falling apart during frying.
4. In a deep frying pan or kadhai, heat enough ghee or coconut oil over medium-low heat for frying. Make sure the oil is not too hot, as it can cause the gulab jamun to brown too quickly without cooking through.
5. Gently add the balls to the heated oil, frying them in batches to avoid overcrowding the pan. Cook the gulab jamun balls until golden brown, turning them occasionally to ensure even cooking.
6. Once cooked, remove the fried balls from the oil and drain on a paper towel to remove excess oil.
7. In a separate saucepan, combine water, powdered erythritol, rose water, and crushed cardamom pods. Bring the mixture to a boil, then reduce the heat and simmer for about 10 minutes to allow the flavors to infuse. Remove from heat and let it cool slightly.
8. Carefully dip the fried gulab jamun balls into the warm syrup, ensuring they are completely submerged. Allow them to soak for at least 15-20 minutes, or until they become moist and tender.
9. Serve the keto-friendly Gulab Jamun warm or at room temperature, garnished with a sprinkle of crushed pistachios or almonds. Enjoy this delightful Indian dessert while staying true to your ketogenic lifestyle.

Note: The syrup quantity can be adjusted based on personal preference. If you prefer a less sweet dessert, reduce the amount of syrup used or soak the gulab jamun for a shorter duration.

Savor the rich, aromatic flavors of this low-carb Gulab Jamun, a beloved Indian dessert. Indulge in the soft and moist texture, fragrant with cardamom and rose water, while reveling in the delight of a keto-friendly treat that won't derail your health goals.

Saffron Almond Keto Barfi

Ingredients:
- 1 cup almond flour
- 1/4 cup powdered erythritol or your preferred sugar substitute
- 1/4 cup unsalted butter, melted
- 1/4 teaspoon cardamom powder
- A pinch of saffron strands
- 2 tablespoons sliced almonds, for garnish

Instructions:
1. In a non-stick pan, heat the almond flour over low heat, stirring constantly for 3-4 minutes. This helps toast the flour slightly and enhances the nutty flavour. Be careful not to burn it.
2. In a mixing bowl, combine the toasted almond flour, powdered erythritol, melted butter, cardamom powder, and saffron strands. Mix well until everything is thoroughly combined and the mixture resembles a crumbly dough.
3. Transfer the mixture to a square or rectangular baking dish lined with parchment paper. Spread and press the mixture evenly into the dish, ensuring it is compacted.
4. Garnish the top with sliced almonds, gently pressing them into the surface of the barfi mixture.
5. Place the dish in the refrigerator and allow it to chill for at least 2-3 hours or until the barfi becomes firm.
6. Once chilled and firm, remove the barfi from the dish and cut it into small squares or desired shapes.
7. Serve the saffron almond keto barfi as a delightful and guilt-free Indian dessert. Enjoy the nutty richness, fragrant aromas, and the subtle sweetness, all without compromising your ketogenic lifestyle.

Note: Store the saffron almond keto barfi in an airtight container in the refrigerator for up to 1 week. Bring it to room temperature before serving for the best texture and flavor.

Experience the luxurious combination of saffron and almonds in this keto-friendly twist on traditional Indian barfi. With its melt-in-your-mouth goodness, subtle sweetness, and delightful aroma, this saffron almond keto barfi is a perfect treat for any occasion. Indulge in the pleasure of a sweet Indian dessert while staying true to your ketogenic journey.

Coconut Laddoos with Stevia

Ingredients:
- 2 cups unsweetened shredded coconut
- 1/2 cup powdered stevia or your preferred sugar substitute
- 1/4 cup heavy cream
- 1/2 teaspoon cardamom powder
- 1/4 teaspoon rose water (optional)
- A pinch of saffron strands (optional)
- Sliced almonds or pistachios, for garnish

Instructions:
1. In a non-stick pan, toast the shredded coconut over low heat for 4-5 minutes until it turns golden brown and gives off a fragrant aroma. Ensure you stir continuously to prevent burning.
2. In a mixing bowl, combine the toasted shredded coconut, powdered stevia, heavy cream, cardamom powder, rose water (if using), and saffron strands (if using). Mix well until all the ingredients are thoroughly combined and the mixture holds together.
3. Allow the mixture to cool slightly, making it easier to handle.
4. Take a small portion of the mixture and firmly press it together to form a small ball or laddoo shape. Repeat this process with the remaining mixture.
5. Garnish each laddoo with a sliced almond or pistachio on top, gently pressing it into the surface.
6. Place the coconut laddoos on a serving tray and refrigerate for at least 30 minutes to allow them to firm up and set.
7. Serve the coconut laddoos as a delightful keto-friendly Indian dessert. Enjoy the rich coconut flavor, the aromatic hints of cardamom, and the delightful sweetness, all without compromising your commitment to a low-carb lifestyle.

Note: Store the coconut laddoos in an airtight container in the refrigerator for up to one week. Allow them to come to room temperature before serving for the best texture and flavor.

Experience the traditional joy of coconut laddoos with this keto-friendly adaptation that brings the same delicious flavors with a lower carbohydrate impact. These delightful coconut laddoos with stevia are perfect for festive occasions or as a sweet treat to satisfy your cravings while maintaining your ketogenic lifestyle. Enjoy the rich, sweet, and nutty essence of Indian desserts without derailing your health goals.

Keto-friendly Indian Rice Pudding

Ingredients:
- 1 cup cauliflower rice
- 2 cups unsweetened almond milk
- 1/4 cup powdered erythritol or your preferred sugar substitute
- 1/4 teaspoon cardamom powder
- 1/4 teaspoon ground cinnamon
- 1/4 cup sliced almonds, for garnish
- 1 tablespoon unsalted pistachios, chopped, for garnish

Instructions:
1. In a saucepan, combine the cauliflower rice and almond milk. Bring the mixture to a gentle simmer over medium heat.
2. Reduce the heat to low and continue cooking, stirring occasionally, for about 10-15 minutes or until the cauliflower rice is tender and the mixture thickens slightly.
3. Add the powdered erythritol, cardamom powder, and ground cinnamon to the saucepan. Stir well to combine and continue cooking for another 5 minutes to allow the flavors to meld together.
4. Remove the saucepan from the heat and let the rice pudding cool slightly. It will thicken further as it cools.
5. Transfer the rice pudding to serving bowls or glasses. Allow it to chill in the refrigerator for at least 1-2 hours to firm up.
6. Prior to serving, garnish the keto-friendly Indian rice pudding with sliced almonds and chopped pistachios.
7. Serve the rice pudding chilled and savor the creamy and comforting flavors reminiscent of the classic Indian dessert, while keeping your carbohydrate intake in check.

Note: If you prefer a sweeter pudding, you can adjust the amount of powdered erythritol or your preferred sugar substitute to taste. Additionally, you can experiment with adding a pinch of saffron strands or a splash of rose water for a delightful twist.

Enjoy the velvety texture, warming spices, and the essence of traditional Indian rice pudding in this keto-friendly adaptation. Indulge in the creamy goodness while staying true to your ketogenic lifestyle. This satisfying and delicate dessert is the perfect way to end a meal or treat yourself to a sweet delight without compromising your health goals.

Spice Up Your Sip: Keto Indian Beverages

Get ready to quench your thirst and indulge your taste buds with a delightful selection of keto-friendly Indian beverages. In this chapter, we explore the world of Indian drinks, showcasing a range of refreshing and flavourful options that align with the principles of the ketogenic diet.

Beverages play a vital role in Indian culinary traditions, offering cooling relief from the tropical heat and a burst of lively flavours to accompany meals. From the fragrant and aromatic Masala Chai to the refreshing Nimbu Pani, we bring you a collection of keto-friendly twists on beloved Indian drinks.

In this chapter, we present four meticulously crafted recipes that combine the authentic essence of Indian beverages with low-carb ingredients. Each recipe is designed to tantalize your taste buds, providing a remarkable fusion of traditional flavours and the nutritional benefits of the ketogenic lifestyle.

Experience the warmth and comfort of a hot cup of Keto-friendly Masala Chai, infusing aromatic spices like cardamom, cinnamon, and ginger into a creamy blend of tea and coconut milk. Or sip on the delightful Keto Lassi with Mixed Berries, a refreshing and creamy beverage made with Greek yogurt, mixed berries, and a touch of sweetness from Stevia.

Indulge in the golden hues of Golden Spiced Keto Milk, a comforting and nourishing drink that combines the goodness of turmeric, ginger, and cinnamon with creamy coconut milk. And don't forget to try the zesty and refreshing Keto-friendly Nimbu Pani, a classic Indian lemonade, elevated with a dash of black salt and a hint of mint.

Whether you are looking for a morning pick-me-up, a refreshing drink to accompany your meal, or simply a way to satisfy your cravings, these keto-friendly Indian beverages offer a delightful and health-conscious solution. Each recipe has been carefully tailored to fit within the guidelines of the ketogenic diet while capturing the authentic flavours that make Indian beverages so renowned.

So, grab your ingredients, prepare your glasses, and get ready to sip your way through the vibrant and invigorating world of Indian beverages adapted for the ketogenic lifestyle. Join us as we showcase the art of balancing flavours, aromas, and nutrients in this exciting chapter of Curry on the Keto: A Low-Carb Twist on Indian Food.

Keto-friendly Masala Chai

Ingredients:
- 2 cups water
- 2 black tea bags (or 2 teaspoons loose black tea leaves)
- 1 cup unsweetened almond milk (or any keto-friendly milk substitute)
- 2 tablespoons heavy cream
- 1-inch piece of fresh ginger, peeled and crushed
- 2-3 green cardamom pods, lightly crushed
- 1 cinnamon stick
- 1-2 teaspoons powdered erythritol or your preferred keto-friendly sweetener (optional)
- Pinch of ground nutmeg (optional)
- Pinch of ground cloves (optional)
- Pinch of ground black pepper (optional)

Instructions:
1. In a saucepan, bring the water to a boil.
2. Add the crushed ginger, cardamom pods, and cinnamon stick to the boiling water. Allow it to simmer for 5 minutes to infuse the flavours.
3. Reduce the heat to low and add the tea bags or loose tea leaves. Let it steep for another 2-3 minutes.
4. Remove the saucepan from heat and add the almond milk, heavy cream, and your preferred keto-friendly sweetener (if using). Stir well to combine.
5. Return the saucepan to low heat and gently warm the chai for 2-3 minutes.
6. Using a fine-mesh strainer, strain the chai into serving mugs, discarding the spices and tea leaves.
7. Sprinkle a pinch of ground nutmeg, cloves, and black pepper (if using) on top of each cup for an extra aromatic touch.
8. Serve the keto-friendly Masala Chai hot and enjoy the comforting and spiced flavours of this iconic Indian beverage.

Indulge in the warmth and fragrance of this keto-friendly adaptation of Masala Chai, where the aromatic blend of ginger, cardamom, and cinnamon is perfectly balanced with creamy almond milk. This energizing and flavourful beverage is the perfect way to start your morning or enjoy a comforting cuppa throughout the day.

Sip and savour the delightful fusion of Indian flavours and the principles of the ketogenic diet as you explore the variety of keto-friendly Indian beverages featured in this chapter. From morning awakenings to evening refreshments, these recipes will bring a touch of India to your keto journey.

Keto Lassi with Mixed Berries

Ingredients:
- 1 cup unsweetened Greek yogurt
- 1/2 cup mixed berries (such as strawberries, blueberries, raspberries)
- 1/2 cup unsweetened almond milk (or any keto-friendly milk substitute)
- 1 tablespoon heavy cream
- 1/2 teaspoon vanilla extract
- 1-2 teaspoons powdered erythritol or your preferred keto-friendly sweetener (optional)
- Ice cubes, for serving
- Mint leaves, for garnish (optional)

Instructions:
1. In a blender, combine the Greek yogurt, mixed berries, almond milk, heavy cream, vanilla extract, and your preferred keto-friendly sweetener (if using).
2. Blend until smooth and well combined, ensuring the berries are fully blended.
3. Taste and adjust the sweetness as desired by adding more sweetener, if needed.
4. Add a few ice cubes to the blender and pulse briefly to incorporate and chill the lassi.
5. Pour the keto Lassi into serving glasses and garnish with mint leaves, if desired.
6. Serve cold and enjoy the refreshing and creamy flavours of this keto-friendly twist on a beloved Indian beverage.

Experience the delightful combination of creamy yogurt, mixed berries, and a touch of sweetness in this keto Lassi with Mixed Berries. This refreshing beverage is the perfect way to cool down on a warm day or enjoy as a creamy treat between meals, all while staying true to your ketogenic lifestyle.

Savour the fusion of traditional Indian flavours with low-carb ingredients as you explore the diverse range of keto-friendly Indian beverages in this chapter. From energizing spiced teas to comforting creamy concoctions, these recipes will add a delightful twist to your keto journey.

Keto-friendly Nimbu Pani

Ingredients:
- 2 lemons
- 4 cups of water
- 1/4 teaspoon of black salt
- 1/4 teaspoon of pink Himalayan salt
- 2 teaspoons of stevia or your preferred keto-friendly sweetener
- Ice cubes
- Fresh mint leaves (optional, for garnish)

Instructions:
1. Juice the lemons into a bowl, removing any seeds.
2. In a pitcher, combine the lemon juice, water, black salt, pink Himalayan salt, and stevia. Stir well to ensure the salt and sweetener are evenly distributed.
3. Taste the nimbu pani and adjust the sweetness or saltiness according to your preference.
4. Fill glasses with ice cubes and pour the nimbu pani over the ice.
5. Garnish with fresh mint leaves, if desired.
6. Serve chilled and enjoy the refreshing and tangy keto-friendly nimbu pani on a hot day!

Note: You can also add a pinch of roasted cumin powder for an extra burst of flavor if desired. Remember to adjust the quantity according to your taste preferences.

Keto-friendly Masala Chaas

Ingredients:
- 1 cup plain full-fat yogurt
- 1 cup water
- 1/4 teaspoon roasted cumin powder
- 1/4 teaspoon pink Himalayan salt
- 1/4 teaspoon black pepper
- A pinch of black salt (optional)
- 1/2 teaspoon grated ginger
- 1 green chili, finely chopped (optional)
- Fresh mint leaves, for garnish
- Ice cubes

Instructions:
1. In a blender or mixing bowl, combine the yogurt, water, roasted cumin powder, pink Himalayan salt, black pepper, black salt, grated ginger, and chopped green chili (if using). Blend or whisk until well combined and creamy.
2. Taste the masala chaas and adjust the salt and spices according to your preference.
3. Place a few ice cubes into serving glasses.
4. Pour the masala chaas over the ice cubes.
5. Garnish with fresh mint leaves.
6. Serve chilled and enjoy the refreshing and tangy keto-friendly masala chaas as a cooling summer drink or a side accompaniment to your meal.

Note: You can also add a squeeze of lemon or a sprinkle of chaat masala for additional tanginess and flavor. Customize the spiciness by adjusting the amount of green chili according to your taste preferences.

Keeping up with the Keto Lifestyle in an Indian Kitchen

Congratulations on completing your journey through "Curry on the Keto: A Low-Carb Twist on Indian Food"! We hope this recipe book has inspired you to explore the possibilities of Indian cuisine within the framework of the ketogenic lifestyle. As we conclude our culinary adventure, let's recap some key takeaways and practical tips for maintaining the Keto Lifestyle in an Indian kitchen.

First and foremost, remember that the ketogenic diet is not just a temporary fix, but a long-term approach to health and well-being. It is not about depriving yourself of delicious food; it's about making conscious choices and finding creative ways to enjoy the flavours you love while aligning with your dietary goals.

Continue to embrace mindful ingredient choices. Whether it's opting for low-carb alternatives to traditional ingredients or embracing healthy fats, be thoughtful in your selections. Explore the wealth of keto-friendly Indian recipes available and experiment with ingredient substitutions that suit your taste and dietary needs.

Practice portion control and mindful eating. Even when following a ketogenic diet, it's important to listen to your body's hunger and fullness signals. Pay attention to portion sizes and savour each bite, allowing yourself to truly enjoy the culinary delights you create.

Continue to educate yourself on the ketogenic diet and Indian cuisine. Stay curious and explore the ever-evolving landscape of nutritional science. Seek out information on new ingredient substitutes, cooking techniques, or creative ways to enjoy your favourite Indian dishes while staying true to the principles of the ketogenic lifestyle.

Remember that balance is key. While the ketogenic diet offers numerous benefits, it's important to find a balance between your dietary goals and your cultural background. Indian cuisine is deeply rooted in tradition and cultural identity, and it's essential to honour that while adapting to a healthier lifestyle. Incorporate occasional indulgences or modifications that still allow you to enjoy your favourite festival meals or family recipes.

Finally, don't be afraid to experiment and make the ketogenic lifestyle your own. Modify recipes, create your own signature dishes, or share your adaptations with friends and family. The power of food is not just in its nourishment but also in the joy it brings when shared with loved ones.

Thank you for joining us on this culinary adventure. We hope "Curry on the Keto: A Low-Carb Twist on Indian Food" has served as a reliable guide in your kitchen, inspiring you to redefine what it means to balance health and tradition. Remember, the ketogenic lifestyle is not a one-size-fits-all approach, and it's essential to listen to your body and adapt as needed.

May your journey towards optimal health and flavourful meals be filled with joy, discovery, and a delicious abundance of Indian-inspired ketogenic delights. Curry on and keto on!

Printed in Great Britain
by Amazon